Pr

Mad

MW00490475

"Holly Otten has done ⌐ ⌐
that will challenge and inspire you to another level on
your Christian journey. As you read her stories of how
the love and fire of God came in like a flood, you can
feel your faith rise up to experience the power of these
real-life testimonies This book will rock you and move
you to the core! *Made for Love* is a book of love that
only could have been written by the tender hand of one
who has lived it—one who loves deeply. I look forward
to more books from this abandoned-to-the-One author."
~Dotty Ellingwood, *Sr. Pastor, RI Genesis Church*

"In *Made for Love,* Holly portrays the very essence of
the love of God in this captivating compilation of
testimonies. In this book you will observe how the love
of the Father brings His lost and broken children from
bondage to breakthrough; and tremendous healing to
the mind, body, soul and spirit. You will learn through
Holly's life's lessons and profound spiritual revelations,
to have life—life in abundance. I consider *Made for Love*
a guide to love. It will leave you knowing the love of the
God in a whole new way. Be prepared to go to a new
level of glory in your life!
~Pastor Gina Russo, *Broken Chains Ministries*

"I could think of no person more qualified to write on
the subject of love than Holly. She is a laid-down lover
of Jesus and leaks His love wherever she goes. She is a
woman who has been tested in the fire but she has come
out on the other side with a crazy understanding of how

much "Daddy" God loves her. Holly walks in this revelation in a powerful way! *Made for Love* is a book about her journey with God that will radically transform you. These are not just words on a page. You will receive an impartation of love as you dive in and read it. I promise that you will never be the same again."
~David Paul Bierkan, *Connecticut*

"From the first day I walked into church and witnessed Holly worshipping the Lord, I knew she was a powerful woman of God. The one thing that I've observed in Holly is that she is all about love. She spreads God's love to everyone she meets. In *Made for Love*, the chapter "His Bride" brought me to my knees in tears. I once again fell so intimately and deeply in love with Jesus. I pray that as you read this book, you also will have a love encounter with Him."
~Lee Ann Jaindl, *Rhode Island*

Dedication

I dedicate this book to my Heavenly Father;
my Savior Jesus Christ;
Holy Spirit.

I am indebted to my God for saving me,
healing me, and for setting me free
from the chains of my past.
He loved me like no other and so
I shall follow Him all of the days of my life.
He allowed me to live out my dreams and has given me
new dreams for my future.
They are His dreams for my life, and I say "Yes" to all
that He has destined for me to do,
all for the sake of His Kingdom.
I love Him more than life itself.

I say "Thank You"
"I love You"
To my Lord, my God and my All.

Made for Love

HOLLY OTTEN

ISBN 978-0-692-62648-1

Text and Cover Design
By Holly Otten, unless otherwise noted.

Printed in the United States.

Front Cover: Stephen Forcino

Contents

* Note-Names have been changed to keep anonymity.

Preface

Liquid Love

One evening while worshipping God in church, I heard myself pray "Make our hearts like Yours." I then saw a vision of what you could describe as candle-making. I saw a bunch of small, empty heart molds. Then I saw a large heart filled with melted wax that was being poured into the heart molds. I knew the large heart represented God's heart and the wax was like "liquid love."

God spoke to me about this image. It is His desire to pour His love into our hearts and then for us to pour His love into others. We must be careful that our wax doesn't harden, because if it does, then we wouldn't be able to pour it out. The thing that keeps wax in liquid form is heat or warmth. We mustn't allow our hearts to get cold and hard. We must pray continually for the fire of God's love to burn inside of us.

"Eat, friends and drink.
Drink your fill of love."
Song of Solomon 5:1

"God's love has been
Poured out into our hearts
through the Holy Spirit
who has been given to us."
Romans 5:5

"This is my commandment, that you love one another as I have loved you. Greater love has no one than this, that someone lay down his life for his friends."
John 15:12,13

Chapter One

Hugs Heal

I was talking with a woman with whom I had just met while standing in line at Dunkin Donuts. She and her six children had made this pit stop on their way to Maine. She was sharing with me that she had packed up her kids and left her abusive husband behind in Texas. While she was sharing, I felt that God the Father was prompting me to wrap my arms around her in a hug. I didn't act on it though, at least not yet.

We continued to talk as we each ordered our coffees. As we turned to walk toward the exit door, I said to her, "I feel that God the Father wants me to give you a hug. May I?" She agreed, and so we placed our coffee cups on the condiment counter, and I wrapped my arms around her—this broken and desperate daughter of the Most High God. I held her closely and not just for a second. I held on long enough so that God's love would be poured in through the words that He gave me and also through the warmth of my embrace. When separated, I said to her apologetically (for doing such a strange thing) "I just felt that He wanted to use my arms to give you a hug." She replied, "Not only that, but He also healed my heart." She then turned and walked out of the door.

As I walked out of Dunkin Donuts, I was thinking "Can God heal a person's heart with a hug? In only a matter of minutes?" Then my mind wandered to the biblical story found in Mark Five[1] when the woman with the issue of blood was healed with only one touch...in a single second.

What does a hug say? A hug says to me, "You are not alone. You are safe. You are loved. You are valued." When we wrap our arms around a person in the name of the Father, His love is able to pass through us just like a conduit. As our arms embrace another in His name, we are causing that person to feel what is in God's heart for them—that He loves them; that they are safe, and that they are not alone.

I learned of the importance of a hug or touch when I studied child psychology in college. I was asked to read in my text book about Harry Harlow who studied the "Science of Love and the Nature of Affection." On an experiment with monkeys, he learned that they preferred contact and comfort from a surrogate mother over food. This particular study made an impact on me at that time in my life. It caused me to reflect upon my own experiences. I was not comfortable hugging or being hugged by others. I much preferred to stay at arm's length with all people, including family members. I learned at an early age that touch is a bad thing; that touches can hurt you and scar you for life. I learned this from the people who sexually abused me as a child.

On the other hand, I also learned at an early age that the *lack* of touch can hurt. My mother was going through a crisis in her marriage when I was in my first years and therefore she wasn't able to be there for me emotionally. She was also forced to work several jobs to provide for me and my siblings, so she wasn't there for me physically. I later learned how much this hurt me, when in my twenties, I experienced a flashback in a therapy session. I cried out with tears streaming down my face, "Don't put me down. Don't leave me," over and over. I saw myself as a baby being placed into a crib. All that I could feel in that moment was the desire to be held; to be cooed over; to be caressed and to be made to feel that I was special. The lack of receiving love and affection through touch caused me to not feel safe or valued. It became the reason why I grew up seeking the affections of men as a teenager. I never did receive from them what I so yearned for. The only one who was able to give me all that my parents and boyfriends couldn't is God.

The Bible says that God is love. It also says that we are created in His image. I believe that God created us to love and be loved. When babies are born and are not given "hugs" or affection, they can be diagnosed with what the medical experts call "Failure to thrive." *Failure to thrive* is when a person (most common in babies and the elderly) falls below the threshold of physical affection needed to stimulate the production of growth hormone and the immune system, and consequently, the body starts shutting down. It is a known fact that babies in orphanages have been known to die from *failure to thrive*, especially in third world countries where the number of orphans is high and the number of staff is low. Author Maia Szalavitz wrote an article entitled "How Orphanages Kill Babies." She states that "they die from lack of love." She goes on to explain that "babies' brains expect that they will experience nearly constant physical touch, rocking and cuddling; without it, they just don't grow."

Renowned child psychologist Bruce Perry shares the same beliefs as Szalavitz. In their book "Born to Love-Why Empathy is Essential and Endangered," Perry emphasizes the need for children to have human contact and experience deep relationships. He believes that this fosters an essential foundation for empathy, and a caring healthy society. He feels that difficulties related to empathy are key factors in social problems such as war, crime, racism, and mental illness. In addition, he states "Even physical health, from infectious diseases to heart attacks, is deeply affected by our human connections to one another."

So there you have it! Scientific proof that hugs heal! They not only heal emotions, but they also heal bodies! I just might have prevented a heart attack last week with a hug! I was visiting a friend who was visibly stressed out. I sat down with her and listened to a long list of things that were going on in her life that were filling her with distress and anxiety. I didn't know what to say to her when she was through. Everything within me wanted to take away all of her problems. My response came in the form of a hug. I got up and wrapped my arms around her. I held on tightly, and as I did, I felt her deflate—more and more with each moment. It was as if pressure was being released. I could feel it physically! My friend became lighter. She was no longer weighed down with burdens in that moment. As I held her, I got an image in my mind's eye of a father carrying a little girl, his daughter, in his arms. I knew what Daddy God was saying...that He was carrying my friend in His arms. Through this gesture He was saying "You are not alone. I am with you. I got you. Everything is going to be OK."

Notes

1. Mark 5:25-34
2. Bruce Perry and Maia Szalavitz. *Born for Love*. Harper Collins. 2011

"For if you love those who love you what recompense will you have?"
Matthew 5:45

Chapter Two

Loving the Unlovely

I truly believed that no one could or would ever love me. I believed I was unlovable. The ones whom I belonged to; who brought me into this world didn't love me. Mom neglected me and Dad abused me. As I grew up, I made it a point to not get too close to anyone, as they might come to know the truth about me; that I was not loveable. Just when I started to feel something deep within my heart for a boyfriend or girlfriend, I sabotaged the relationship by acting mean and abusive, or by disappearing from their lives forever. Subconsciously I thought "If I stay around, I will come to love him deeply and then as soon as he gets to know the real me, which is ugly and unlovely, he will leave me and my heart will be crushed." I couldn't let that happen. My heart was already battered and bruised, and barely survived those early years.

When I became a Christian, I found myself not behaving as one. I told God "You command me to love my neighbor as myself, but I don't know how to love." "What is love?" I often wondered. I didn't know how to receive love nor did I know how to give love. I didn't love myself. Deep down, I hated myself. Often in my prayers, I cried out to God, "Teach me how to love and be loved." Whenever I was baptized by the Holy Spirit (three times in three years), we were told to ask for the gifts of the Spirit. Some asked for the charismatic gifts such as healing and prophecy. The greatest desire of my heart was to be filled with love—one of the nine fruits of the Spirit. Over and over, throughout the years, it has been my prayer, "Give me more love Lord."

God did pour in His love and the proof is that I was able to love a man to the extent of committing my life in marriage. I knew it would have to be a miracle of God to get me to that place of loving and trusting a man, especially after being abused by several men throughout my childhood. It was His love that made it so. More proof is that I was able to love and nurture three children. I never thought that I would be able to do that. Upon receiving the news that I was pregnant with each child, I would shed tears because I feared that I wasn't capable of loving my child in the way that I should. God's love made it possible.

Since I've come to know His love, God always calls me deeper. I've been challenged to love not only the one who is kind to me or who loves me, but the one who is mean to me and hurts me. I remember God calling me to love my father who sexually abused me and denied it. God told me to love him in a tangible way, as if he never harmed me at all. I am to love my father unconditionally; the same way that God loves me. When my confused son was a teen and struggling with his identity, I was the subject of the negative feelings that tormented him. I was treated with hatred and disdain by my son whom I had loved and cared for. At times I would scream at him in the midst of confrontations and say things out of anger that I would later regret. In the midst of this difficult season, I cried out to God, "Help!" I heard Him reply, "Love him." "OK Lord. Give me more love."

In this season of my life, God has called me to minister His love beyond the limits of family. He is calling me to share His love to the broken ones—the unlovely ones—the ones who appear to be unlovable—the ones who have been neglected, abandoned, used up, and abused. These are the toughest ones to love because their hearts have become hardened. The high cement walls have been erected like fortresses to keep out further pain and disappointment. They behave as a wounded animal in the wild that strikes out at you just in case you're thinking of hurting it. This I understand well and I am filled with compassion, because I was once like them.

Sometimes these broken ones keep you at a distance with their outward appearance. God called me to love a woman who grew up in the foster care system. As a small child, her father sexually abused her and her mother was a drug addict. This precious one grew up feeling unlovely inside, so she became unlovely on the outside. She didn't take care of herself and kept people away by choosing to be smelly. She chose not to take care of personal hygiene, nor did she choose to wash her clothes regularly. She made the choice to overeat and not exercise, and so she became obese. Once she was living on her own, she became a hoarder; collecting old and used up things, which most would consider garbage. This behavior kept people from visiting her in her home. Over the years that I've known this woman, I have observed her choices. She doesn't choose to lash out to keep others away. I've never heard her say a mean thing or act in an unkind way to anyone. She is entirely able to bathe herself and clean up after herself. She just chooses not to. This is her method to keep from being hurt or further disappointed.

My compassion for the broken led me to minister in a home for unwed mothers, where ninety-five percent experienced childhood sexual abuse. Half of the girls (average age was seventeen) came to the home because their parents gave an ultimatum: have an abortion or move out. These girls whom God called me to love were wounded and afraid. They feared getting hurt again, so they often pushed me away by hurting me or attacking me with their words.

A girl named Julia gave me the hardest time in the year of my ministry in the home. She acted as if she hated me almost from the day she arrived. Day after day, week after week, she treated me with disrespect and spoke badly about me to the other girls. I was finding it very difficult to love Julia. I went to my Christian friends several times asking for their prayers that God would give me what I needed in order to love her. I knew that I could not do it in my own strength. On one occasion, God led me to give her my gold ring that I wore faithfully, without ever taking it off. Eventually, Julia started coming with me to prayer meetings at my church. I watched her heart soften toward me and it felt so good to see God's love beginning to flow out of her. It was a blessed occasion when Julia invited me to her son's baptism months after she left the home.

I had many opportunities in that year of ministry to love the unlovely. I was called to love the one who made a call to DCYF and accused me of sexually abusing her. I was forced to sit with investigators and answer their questions regarding my actions toward this resident—a broken one. I cried out to God for truth to prevail and then I cried out for more love. I knew that He called me to forgive and to love this broken one unconditionally. On another occasion, a resident stole from my closet a summer white dress with the tag still attached. I wanted this former stripper to feel beautiful, pure and lovely, so I never said a word about it to anyone. On the day that she left the home I gave her my own gold necklace with a cross pendant. The best thing about that was that she *received* it. She wanted it. She wanted what the cross represented-LOVE. While living in the home, she came to know Jesus who lives in me and who loved her unconditionally, through me.

That year was not an easy one! It was very difficult to continuously love those who did not love me in return. It was difficult to not get satisfaction from vengeance or vindication every time I was wronged or falsely accused. It was also humbling. I had to lay down my pride or the need to be right, for the sake of love. I had to remind myself of the reasons behind their actions and therefore, to not take things personally. Over time, as I forgave each offense and continued to love them anyway, they began to learn the truth...That they *were* lovable! And as they received love, they were better able to give it away.

When I was young the devil lied to me. He told me that I was unlovable. The truth is...WE WERE MADE TO LOVE! God, who is love itself, created us in His image. In other words: Love created you and me to love and be loved. I want to make it my mission in life, for the rest of my years, to undo what the devil has done. I want to live my life in a way that reveals the truth to those who have believed the lie that they are unlovable and unlovely. By God's grace, I will do it.

[27]

"Now this is our boast: Our conscience testifies that we have conducted ourselves in the world, and especially in our relations with you, with integrity and godly sincerity."
1 Corinthians 1:12

Chapter Three

Transparency

Two weeks ago my "BFFs" and I were praying together when one said "I see you Holly, but all I can see is a skeleton." "Yikes!" I thought. "That image is creepy." I asked God what He was saying and then the image of an x-ray photograph came to my mind. When a doctor examines the picture of an x-ray, he is able to see past the outer layers of the body and into the core, the skeleton. The inner part of the body is no longer hidden. The condition of the bones is revealed.

Yesterday I was shopping in Walmart and my eyes fell upon a woman's t-shirt. I instantly knew that God was speaking to me through that shirt. It depicted an x-ray view of the chest with white skeletal ribs, but in addition, it had a bright red heart. I immediately thought of the vision my friend had got of me as a skeleton. As I sought God and asked Him what He was saying to me, I heard the word "transparency."

God desires that I be transparent. The only thing that He wants people to see when they look at me is my heart. He desires that I have no hidden agendas, masks or pretenses. These things keep people from seeing my heart. They are layers which act as walls that keep people out.

The idea of letting these walls down is a scary one. One becomes vulnerable; open to attack or offenses. I remember feeling this vulnerability when I had gone to an intensive training seminar on inner-healing. I was chosen by the leader to be part of a model inner-healing session. There I sat as the leader took me back to my past; to childhood wounds inflicted by my father who sexually abused me. I literally felt as if I were a child again, feeling all of the feelings associated to that period in my life. I began to cry because of the extreme vulnerability that I felt. I was sitting in front of a group of twenty-five people and I felt as if I were lying on a table completely naked. I felt exposed. My insides were on the outside. Nothing was hidden.

I had this exact feeling several months later when the details of my life were printed on the cover of a newspaper. I willingly agreed to share my life details with a journalist but once I saw my face on the cover for all to see, along with the details of being sexually abused as a child and raped as a teen. I felt as if there was a naked picture of me on that cover. As I looked at the cover, it made me want to grab a blanket and cover myself up. I felt so exposed. As I cried out to God, He spoke a word to me that made me feel that I was covered up. "She is *clothed* with strength and dignity."[1] I was immediately filled with peace.

These two incidents were orchestrated by God. They were experiences that fostered transparency in me. All of the wounds that my heart received as a child caused me to put up walls around my heart. Those walls had to come down in order for me to love others. In addition, God desired for me to help other survivors of sexual abuse receive healing. Since I have published my book "The Tin Man-The Voice of an Incest Survivor" my life's secrets are out for the world to see. I've learned that my transparency helps others to be transparent with me. I've met many people, both men and women, who upon hearing my story feel safe to share theirs with me.

When I am facilitating workshops that lead survivors through the healing process, I experience the same dynamic. For eight weeks I share with women my life experiences of sexual abuse and because I bare my heart to them and expose all of my feelings, they in turn do so with me. Because I have let my guard down, they feel that it is safe to do the same. This fosters healing in them. In this form of transparency, dark secrets are exposed. Shame and guilt fall away. The dirty secrets no longer have a hold on them.

I remember the day that Maria sat down with me to tell me of her dark secret. For thirty-three years she never told a single soul of her secret—not her mother, who was her best friend, nor her husband of five years. She barely knew me but she knew "about me." She thought, "If she has the courage to tell the world, then I can have the courage to tell her." Maria shared with me that she was molested as a child by a neighbor. As she brought this dark secret to the light, she wept. Those tears that were shed washed all of the "dirt" away. Those tears that fell were tears of freedom! She was no longer bound by the lies that it was her fault and that she was shameful. Maria felt free! She was forever changed that night.

When God took me through the process of healing from childhood abuse and neglect, I learned that I had created masks and acted out roles to cover up the truth of who I was deep inside. I almost always wore a mask that made me appear happy. In addition, I had several roles that I played throughout the years. I played the good-girl role (so people wouldn't know that I was bad), the bad-girl role (I believed the lie that I was guilty for what had been done to me), and the party-girl role (I was the life of the party to cover up the truth that I was miserable). I also acted intimidating so that others would think twice about hurting me (Deep down inside I was a wounded and fearful little girl). As God's light shone in my dark places, lies were uncovered and His truths were revealed. I learned that God loved me and accepted me just as I am. I had no more reasons to hide behind masks or pretenses. This gave me a sense of freedom—I was free to be me! I learned "It's OK to be real. It's OK to be me." This is transparency.

Today I have people who meet me and tell me that I am transparent. When I ask them to explain what they mean, they say things like... "You are real." "You are honest." "I don't get the sense that

you are pretending to be someone that you aren't."
"I don't feel that you are hiding anything from me."
Wow! I've come a long way! This is God's doing. It is His work and His grace. It is God's desire for His children to connect at a heart level—heart to heart, with nothing in between—nothing obstructing the matters of the heart. Why live any other way? To live this way is to live life to the fullest!

Notes

1.   Psalms 31:25

*"Now that you have purified yourselves by obeying
the truth so that you have sincere love for each other,
love one another deeply from the heart."*
1 Peter 1:22

Chapter Four

Tenderhearted

I was trying to cut into my cheap piece of filet mignon but was getting nowhere. Since my steak knife wasn't doing the job, I went to the kitchen and got a seven-inch carving knife. I had success in cutting myself a bite-sized piece but once I got it into my mouth, it was like chewing on a piece of leather. The meat was inedible! I immediately got up and threw it in the garbage. Boy did I regret buying that meat from a different store than usual at a cheaper price. As I pondered this, I heard God speak to my heart. He made me aware of an analogy...Just as a hardened piece of steak is not desirable to us, neither are our hardened hearts desirable to God. When we allow our hearts to be hardened, God's love is unable to pass through us, whether to receive it or give it away.

His words reminded me of something that I said to my pastors not so long ago. I said "I feel like my heart is a piece of raw meat that is being tenderized." I literally felt as if my heart was being pounded with a steel mallet just as a tough piece of meat is made tender. My heart was enduring much pain in that time of my life. I was experiencing the loss of one of my sons and also the loss of one of my best friends. My teen son was going through a rough time and was acting out with rebellion and defiance in our home. When he realized that it would not be tolerated, he moved to a house where he could do as he pleased. In my heart, I desired for him to return to our home, be reconciled to us, and live together in mutual love and respect. But it didn't happen as I wished. I cried every day for six weeks. My heart was broken. My son, whom I loved dearly, walked out of my life and wanted nothing to do with me. And all I did was love him. It wasn't right. It wasn't fair. Why was I being treated like the one who did something wrong?

I took my broken heart to God. I unloaded my hurt feelings onto Him—my loving Father and Comforter. As I did, I felt God's love softening my heart. The angry feelings that I felt toward my son were turned into love and forgiveness. This enabled me to love him unconditionally, even though his love was not being returned.

At the very same time that I suffered the loss of my son, I also suffered the loss of a valued friendship. Sophia was one of the few women that I let completely into my heart. All of my life I had kept up a guard around my heart and it kept me from having deep and lasting relationships with men and women. For five years Sophia and I hung out together like chums—like sisters. We laughed together and cried together; dreamed together and prayed together. Whenever I felt that my heart strings were being tugged, I consciously made the decision to allow it. I made the decision to love Sophia with my whole heart, feeling that we would be friends forever.

The loss of Sophia's friendship and the pain that my heart-felt reminded me of the pain from the loss of marriage to my first husband Doug. It was by the grace of God that I opened my heart to love a man with such depth. However, I did have choices to make. I had to choose to let my guard down. I had to choose for my heart to be softened by love. I had to choose to let go of all of the feelings of fear and anger toward the men that abused me earlier in life. At this time in my life I adopted a motto. It is a truth and a promise found in God's Word. "The thief (devil) comes to steal, kill and destroy, but I (Jesus) have come that they would have life and have it to the fullest."[1] I made up my mind then that I would not allow the devil to keep me from having a fulfilling relationship with a man in marriage or from fulfilling relationships with my future children. Nonetheless, after eight years of marriage and giving birth to three boys, my marriage to Doug came to an end. My heart was broken in half. I felt as if a part of me had died.

I may have lost a friend in Sophia and a husband in Doug, but I don't regret for a minute that I loved them with my whole heart. I came to realize that by loving them to the fullest I was living life to the fullest! This is victory for me! And because I did not allow my heart to be hardened when I experienced these losses, I opened my heart to love in new relationships. I know for certain that the devil wanted me to put up those once familiar walls around my heart to keep me from loving and being loved by others. If I did that then I wouldn't have been able to experience the joy in loving my new husband and my new girlfriend! In addition, because I chose to love my son and Sophia unconditionally and forgive them, they have both returned to me and have chosen to love me in return. To love is joy! To love is to live!

Yes, I made the choice a second time to allow my heart to open to another man to the depth of committing my life in marriage. My God is the God of second chances! It was my heart's desire to be a wife and mother before meeting Doug. When that marriage didn't succeed, my heart's desire did not change. On my wedding day, I shared my own personal handwritten vows... "I promise to LIVE *life to the fullest*, to LOVE *unconditionally*, and to LAUGH *until my belly hurts*."

This past August, we celebrated our eighth anniversary over dinner in a five-star restaurant where only the best cuts of meat are served. Of course I ordered my favorite dinner item—filet mignon. Boy did I have a smile on my face when the waitress set my plate before me with a juicy piece of steak in the shape of a perfect heart! I knew that it was a gift from my Daddy God...I knew that He was pleased with me. I had not allowed my heart to be hardened. I chose to love even when that choice in the past brought me pain. I have kept my heart soft and tender. This is the desire of God's heart.

Notes
1. John 10:10
2. Isaiah 61:7

*"We were therefore buried with him
through baptism into death in order that,
just as Christ was raised from the dead
through the glory of the Father,
we too may live a new life."*
Romans 6:4

Chapter Five

Residents of Heaven

As I was thinking about the incident from the day before, I heard God say to me "You behaved as a heavenly woman." Immediately tears fell from my eyes. It wasn't easy—overcoming the flesh—to not let my flesh have its way. My flesh wanted to strangle my adversary—the one who was trying everything in his power to cause me pain. On that day of emotional anguish, I had to face this man for the fifth time in six months and defend myself from his false allegations in the county courthouse. When the session broke for a recess, I immediately broke down in tears. I cried out to God for grace. I was filled with so much frustration regarding this man. I prayed a prayer of forgiveness and released him to God—the ultimate Judge. With everything within me, I made the decision to not hold a grudge against this man.

When court was adjourned, and it came time to speak for myself, the man-appointed judge gave me a choice of whether I wanted to force my opponent to refund me the amount of money that he overcharged me. I made the decision to let go of the debt owed to me. Afterwards, I told a friend of mine what I chose to do and he thought that I had made a bad decision—that money was rightfully mine. However, on the following day, as I talked things over with my Daddy God, He revealed to me, that the decision that I had made showed that I did not hold a grudge toward my opponent. I did not have a spirit of revenge in me. I made a choice that was hard for a person to understand; but my Daddy God understood it. I chose to love instead of hate. I chose peace instead of war. I behaved as a heavenly woman would.

This dying to self is not easy. It is painful. I remember not so long ago, when my friend shared with me a vision that she had of me. She saw me lying down in a casket, with my arms crossed over my chest. Then she saw wings coming out of the sides of the casket. She told me, "As you die to self, God will cause you to fly." It's like Jesus. He modeled this for us. Jesus forfeited the desires of His flesh when He obeyed the Father's command to give His life on the cross. He was buried but then He rose again, and now He sits in the heavens—his forever residence. A few weeks after the vision, God brought me to a place in which I had a choice to die to self. God was convicting me during a Sunday morning service of something that I needed to repent of. He revealed to me an unknown sin. By the closing of the service I made my way to the front. I stood before my church family with a heart filled with repentance and tears flowing down my face. It was humbling to say the least.

Why would God want to humble me that way? It is a process of emptying out self, in order that God's life and glory can live inside of me. As I die, He can live in me. I am reminded of Paul's words..."It is no longer I who live, but Christ who lives in me."[1]

The very first time that God taught me the lesson of dying to self was twenty years ago. I had attended a prayer meeting at a church that was not my own. During the service, God was convicting me of the way that I treated my husband. It was as if God removed the scales that were covering my eyes, which kept me from seeing my actions for what they were. My behavior and words toward my husband were abusive. I was not behaving in a loving way toward my husband and it was not pleasing to God. My sins were like filth before me. I wanted to be made clean again. I wanted to start new. I felt that God was urging me to confess my sin in front of the church body. I went forward, stood before a crowd of two hundred and made a public confession. My sin was there for all to see. In that moment, it was as if my flesh was being killed. This was a good thing. With Holly out of the way, Christ's glory could live in me and shine through me. It is always painful in the moment of dying to self, but in the very next moment there is resurrection life!

God told me that I behaved as a heavenly woman. I've thought a lot about that statement ever since I heard it. If I behave as a heavenly woman, then I'm behaving as a resident of heaven. This leads me to think about how residents of heaven behave. In heaven, there is love instead of hate, peace instead of war, forgiveness instead of vengeance. My prayer is that I think and act as a Christian whose residence is in heaven. If I live and act as a heavenly woman, I just might be mistaken for an angel! God brought this to mind when I gazed on the words of my niece's plaque that hangs on her kitchen wall... "I've seen and met angels wearing the disguise of ordinary people, living super-ordinary lives."

Notes   1. Galatians 2:20

"Love your enemies; do good to those who hate you. Bless those who curse you; pray for those who mistreat you. If someone slaps you on one cheek, turn to them the other also. If someone takes your coat, do not withhold your shirt from them. Give to everyone who asks you, and if anyone takes what belongs to you, do not demand it back."
Luke 6:27-30

Chapter Six

Love Melts Chains

I was crying out to God in prayer for a select few...the one who lost his father in a single moment at the age of thirteen, who from that moment on, blamed God for every bad thing that happened to him for the following thirty-five years...for the six-year-old girl in foster care, who was shuffled around to ten different locations in two years...for the one who was raped repeatedly from the age of four, throughout her teen years, and then again at age fifty. I prayed..."Heal their wounds and melt their frozen hearts with Your love. And pour more of Your love into my heart so that I can love them." Suddenly in my mind's eye, I saw hot, liquid lava pouring down, as if flowing out of the tip of a volcano and down its mountainside. I knew that this hot, liquid love that was flowing from God's heart was hot enough to melt chains...chains of hatred, fear, anger, mistrust and unforgiveness.

I've looked into eyes and have seen hatred looking back at me. I've looked into eyes filled with violence and vengeance. They were the eyes of a wounded one; a hardened one; one who feared to love me because love can bring pain. Defenses went up and offenses were committed in an effort to make me go away. God allows me to see inside their hearts. He allows me to feel their pain. Deep down, they are vulnerable and hurting. As He fills me with compassion and understanding, I am able to love them with His love. Over time, as I continue to apply God's hot liquid love, I see their frozen, hardened hearts melt and their chains fall away. I found this concept in a promise from God. In the book of Proverbs it says, "If your enemy is hungry, give him food to eat. If he is thirsty, give him water to drink. In doing this, you will heap burning coals on his head, and the Lord will reward you."[1] Burning coals are a lot like hot liquid lava...both possess extreme hot temperatures, enough to melt hard and frozen substances.

I've read many books that give step-by-step instructions on how to cast out demons from people. I've also been counseled by others that I should take steps to perform deliverances on the people whom I minister to. But when I ask my Daddy God what I should do when I am dealing with one who is bound by the chains of the devil, I only hear Him say

"Love him," or "Love her." I saw a woman delivered from a chain of unforgiveness just as I kissed her tear-stained cheeks and wiped them dry with my hands. It was love that melted this chain. As her tears were released, so was the demon of unforgiveness.

My friend tells the story of how two women prayed for years for her to be set free from drug addiction. Finally, they convinced her to accompany them back to their home state where they would help her with her recovery. Love drove them thirteen hours, across six states to pick up a woman who was not even family, and with no promise of monetary gain. They arrived to find that she had been smoking crack for two weeks straight. These two laid-down-lovers cleaned her apartment and did her dirty laundry. They packed her suitcase with clean clothes and then escorted her to their van. As she entered inside, she became instantly set free from drug addiction. It was evident because her head was clear as if she hadn't smoked a thing. Within the following days, she never experienced withdrawal symptoms, nor did she crave drugs ever again. My friend goes on with her story to explain how those two women loved her and cared for her every minute of their time together. It was the love and prayers of those women that broke the chain of drug addiction.

One of my favorite stories of how love melts chains is found in an autobiography called "The Heavenly Man."[2] The book tells of an extraordinary account of a demon-possessed man who was bound by many chains (physically and spiritually) and who became free not from a deliverance session but simply from the love of a man named Brother Yun. Yun met this tormented soul while in a Chinese prison, where he lived out the punishment for professing his faith in Jesus Christ. Yun tells of his prison mate whom he refers to as a "precious soul of the Lord," who was awaiting execution for murder. "He was handcuffed behind his back and had chains manacled around his ankles. He spoke filthy words and kept trying to mutilate his body by cutting himself with his ankle chains. He was ferocious and full of hatred." Other prisoners treated him like an animal, kicking and punching him. One man told Yun, "He is not a man, but a devil." Yun replied, "Before we believed in Jesus, we were just like him. We too were like demons...We need to have mercy on this man and treat him as if he was Jesus himself." Yun made a daily effort to show this "precious soul" God's love and he encouraged his cell mates to do the same.

One day the man finally broke down in tears, giving evidence that love had melted his frozen heart. On that day Yun was literally starving from hunger, yet He felt God urging him to give his weekly beloved portion of *mantou* to the bound man. As Yun obeyed God, the man's chains melted off right there and then. The man "dropped off his chair, knelt down on the floor, and wept." He then spoke not as a crazy man, but as a man in his right mind... "Why do you love me like this?...I am a murderer, hated by all men...Why do you love me so much?" The man became eager to receive Jesus in his heart, as he realized that Jesus was the source of love that flowed from Yun's heart and into his own. Yun testifies that the man "had become gentle after his conversion and the whole prison noticed the difference." Alleluia! I will see that man in heaven! They may have killed his body by execution, but his soul lives forever in paradise!

I have come to believe that love is the greatest weapon against the devil. Love defeats every form of evil on this earth. When we come face to face with evil; when we are attacked, harmed, slandered, or offended, may we not give them what they deserve. May we give them mercy instead. May we adopt the motto to "Love the hell out of them" as a dear friend of mine is known to say.

"Mercy triumphs over judgment."
James 2:13

Notes

1. Proverbs 25:21, 22

2. Yun and Paul Hattaway. *The Heavenly Man*. London: Monarch Books. 2002

"For we are God's workmanship, created in Christ Jesus to do good works, which God prepared in advance for us to do."
Ephesians 2:10 NESB

Chapter Seven

Diamonds in the Rough

I was worshipping one evening with my two sisters in the Lord. I was singing and dancing my heart out before Him in the sanctuary just like King David in the Old Testament. I then noticed a sparkle on the carpet so I bent down to see what it was. I picked up the sparkly object and observed what looked like a diamond! I placed it in my pocket and continued in my worship. As I twirled around the sanctuary, I noticed another sparkle. I bent down to pick it up and found that it was another diamond-like stone, but of a different size and shape. I placed it in my pocket along with the first one and continued worshipping the Lord.

The following morning I woke up and remembered the diamonds in my pocket. I emptied out my jean pocket and out fell **three** instead of two! I knew that God was speaking to me but I didn't quite know what He was saying...yet. I placed the diamonds in a jewelry dish on my bureau and kept the ears of my heart open to hear my Daddy God's voice on this issue. A few days later I was walking around my church and praying, when I came upon another diamond that was just sitting alone on a shelf surrounding the sound booth. I picked it up and brought it to my pastor and proceeded to tell her of the four diamonds that God gave to me. (It turned out that they were actually rhinestones which were made to appear as diamonds). It was then that my Daddy God spoke to me. He used my pastor as His mouthpiece and she said to me "God is bringing to you 'diamonds in the rough.' He will use you to polish them and make them beautiful."

Diamonds are not naturally beautiful. In their natural state they are called rough diamonds and have the appearance of glassy rocks or rocks of salt. It is the diamond cutter's job to recognize the value and potential of the rough diamond and cause it to surface. After much hard work of cutting, shaping and polishing, the final product is one of brilliance and beauty. It is then prized and considered to be of great worth. When I think about God's words to me and the analogy of polishing rough diamonds, a Canadian man by the name of Jean Vanier comes to mind. Vanier is a known philosopher, theologian and humanitarian. For decades he has advocated for people with developmental disabilities. He has made it his life's mission to bring out the gifts in these "less than perfect" ones. You could say that he is a "diamond cutter" for the Lord. He has been quoted as saying "To love someone is to show them their beauty, their worth, and their importance."

I believe that God is calling me to be like Vanier—to take the less than perfect ones that He brings to me, the diamonds in the rough, and find their gifts and cause them to shine with brilliance. My beloved pastor is a believer of this principle. I've heard her say countless times, "Bring out the glory in them!" This is one of her life's mottos that she lives by. As a matter of fact, in the three years that I've known her, she has done this very thing with me! She has taken me, a rough diamond, and has looked with God's eyes at what He sees in me—the beauty that is hidden. She has polished me with her prayers and words of encouragement and praise and has caused my beauty to shine on the outside, for all to see.

Yes, it is God's doing. He is the ultimate diamond cutter and He trains willing vessels, His hands and feet, to do the same. If there is any beauty in me, it is because of the work that He has done in me. If there are any gifts in me that are glorious or praiseworthy, it is because He placed them inside of me and brought them out of me. I cannot take any credit for the words that you are reading in this book. I am simply a pen in His hand. The words are coming from Him. If I did not pray this morning and ask Him to use me as His conduit, nothing of consequence would be produced. It would be nothing but ink on a page.

Jesus lived out this principle of bringing the glory out of "not-so-shiny" people. The story of Mary Magdalene is just one example.[1] In the Bible, Mary Magdalene was known to be possessed with seven devils. I believe that when Jesus first laid his eyes on Mary Magdalene, He saw not only a woman who was out of her mind or behaving like a demon(s), He saw the faithful, loyal part of her that was hidden inside. He also saw the great ability that she had to love. After Jesus released His mercy and grace to Mary and cast those demons from her, she became a faithful follower of Jesus—even to the cross. When His beloved disciples (all but one) were hiding out in fear for their lives, Mary's love for and loyalty to Jesus kept her by His side until the moment that He drew his last earthly breath. How beautiful and glorious was she in that moment.

Jesus held her in such high esteem that He chose her to reveal His resurrected body on Easter morning. Oh yes! Mary was gloriously transformed during all of the time she spent with Jesus—*the master* "diamond cutter."

In order for me to see the glory inside of a person, I must ask God to help me to see them with His eyes. They are His creation, so He is the one to ask! In the moment that they were conceived, His gifts, plans and purposes for them were also conceived. When God brings a person into my life to minister His love to, I ask Him to tell me about that person. I open the ears of my heart and wait on Him to show me their gifts and character traits that are beautiful and glorious, but just hidden inside. I ask Him to tell me the plans that He has for that specific person. Once I hear from Him, I share it with them. I tell them what God says about them, which is the opposite of what the devil has been telling them. They need to hear what God says, because what He says is true and is good and fills them with hope. What God says is encouraging and points them in a direction that will lead them to living life to the fullest.

I asked God about one of my sons and He told me that he would be the pastor of his own church. He has also repeatedly highlighted a specific scripture throughout my son's childhood years pertaining to a verse that describes an eagle rising up and soaring.[2] I keep these things in my heart to remind myself and my son of God's plans for him. Whenever I see my son behaving or living as a "turkey," I remind him that he is an eagle. Sometimes in my texts to him, I say "I love you Eagle." Sometimes he and I need to be reminded of God's promises, especially because the devil tries every attempt to steer him away from living out his God-given destiny. When my son tells me he's going to be a CEO in corporate America and make millions of dollars, I turn to God and pray that He will have His way in my son's life; that His plan for him to pastor a church will be brought to fruition is His perfect timing.

When God had me ministering to a woman who lost her health, her money, and her dignity, God told me that He was giving her a new name—Esther. I shared with her the story of Esther from the Bible. I told her that Esther was a poor orphan girl whom God raised up to marry a king and to save her entire nation from death. God took Esther, a diamond in the rough, and made her glorious. She became beautiful inside and out. She was arrayed in royal garments and given an inheritance of great wealth and dignity. She became noble, honorable and a leader of her people. This is what God was saying to this woman. This is what He saw in her. This is what He planned for her. Maybe the plan didn't include marrying a king in the natural, but she is certainly a daughter of the King of kings and has been given a glorious inheritance through the salvation of Jesus Christ. So every so often, I remind her of who she is—whom God says she is, by calling her Esther.

The diamond cutter's job isn't easy. Diamonds are very hard stones and therefore they are not easy to cut and shape. In the same way, God may call us to love or minister to people who seem hard or whose hearts have been hardened. We may be asked to love one who might steal from us, swear at us, take advantage of us and not appreciate all that we do for them. It is very important to not focus on the imperfections or flaws in them, but keep our focus on the parts that are beautiful and promising, so as to emphasize them and bring them out. We are to shine up or polish the good parts of the "diamond." We must remind ourselves who God says they are, and keep His vision for the final "product."

Technically, as Christians, we are all diamonds in the rough. We are all a work in progress—God's workmanship[3]—and we will only be perfect when we take our place in heaven. So, if someone calls you a "diamond in the rough" you can take it as a compliment. It means that at a glance, you may appear common or ordinary, but he recognizes a very precious and valuable potential within you. Let's make it our goal to see one another the way that God, our brilliant creator sees us. Let's adopt my pastor's motto…"To pull the glory out of them."

"Therefore, if anyone cleanses
himself from these things, he will be a vessel for
honor, sanctified, useful to the Master,
prepared for every good work."
2 Timothy 2:20

Notes

1. John 20:11-18; Matthew 27:55,56
2. Isaiah 40:30
3. Ephesians 2:10

.

"Come, I will show you the bride,
the wife of the Lamb."
Revelation 21:9

Chapter Eight

His Bride

By the time she was forty, she was married and divorced four times. Every time she became engaged, she flashed her new diamond ring as if to say, "See how much I am loved!" Each time she got a man to put a ring on her finger and agree to commit his life to her forever, she felt validated and loved. Unfortunately, because she never learned what love looked like as a child, she married men who beat her regularly. After all, she was abused by men as a child, even by the ones who were suppose to love her.

Then there's the little girl whose parents were addicted to crack and left her to care for her own needs. She grew up dreaming of the day when she would meet a man who would take her into his arms and profess his undying love for her. When she was all grown up, she became engaged and spent a year planning for an elaborate wedding. She spent thousands of dollars, working two jobs, to have the best of everything. It was as if she was trying to prove to the world and herself that she is loveable, valuable and beautiful. The truth was that deep down, she felt the opposite. Unfortunately, the man who spoke the words that she dreamed of hearing didn't know how to prove his love through his actions. Within the first year of their marriage, he cheated on her with two other women. She had also learned that he cheated on her with a third woman prior to their wedding.

There is a similar story in the Bible which tells of the Samaritan woman.[1] We are told that she married five times. I believe that she received validation that she was loved each time she heard the words "I do," but within a very short time, the feelings would wear off and she would seek to be validated yet again in the arms of another man. When she met Jesus at the well in Samaria, she accepted His offer to drink of His life-giving water and at last, her insatiable desire for love was quenched.

When we were created by God, He placed an empty "well" inside of us that could only be filled with His love. No one and nothing can ever fill that empty place. Many of us live for decades trying to fill the empty well within with the love of people or of things. For the first half of my life I tried filling my "well" with drugs and alcohol, money, pretty things, popularity, and countless men. I too longed to hear those words "I love you" and "You are beautiful" from earthly men, so as to validate my self-worth. None was able to satisfy me until I met Jesus, the lover of my soul. When I opened my heart to the King of love, I was swept off my feet! I would go anywhere and to do anything for the One who made me feel loved like no other.

This type of love affair—Jesus' love for us and our love for Him—is described in the Bible in the Song of Solomon. In this book I learn of His love for me and I hear Him tell me the things that I longed to hear my whole life..."Ah, you are beautiful My beloved...Arise, My beloved, My beautiful one and come!"[1] and then I read the words that are found in my heart for Him..."My lover belongs to me and I to Him...I took hold of Him and would not let Him go."[2] The analogy in this book of King Solomon and a Shulamite woman depicts love in the context of courtship, a wedding, and marriage. The Bible is full of analogies which represent Jesus as a bridegroom who eagerly awaits meeting His bride at the wedding banquet. We, the church, are the bride that our beloved Jesus longs for.

Jesus Himself told a parable about a wedding banquet. He said, "The kingdom of heaven is like a king who prepared a wedding banquet for his son."[3] God the Father is preparing the church, the bride, to marry His Son, the bridegroom. If we want to live happily ever after, feasting on the finest things, then we need to prepare ourselves for the bridegroom and for the wedding celebration.

What does a bride do to prepare for her wedding? A wedding is a celebration of love, so first and foremost, the bride's heart needs to be filled with love for the groom, and it also needs to be fully open to receive his love. She must be prepared to devote her heart to him and him alone; not putting any other loves before him. On the morning of her wedding day she prepares herself. She goes through great efforts to present herself as beautifully as possible. She prepares to clothe herself with the white gown that represents her purity. She makes certain that she is clean and smelling lovely before she dresses herself. She looks the gown over first, because she wants it to be spotless and without any wrinkles. If there is the slightest blemish, she is quick to apply a cleaning solvent to be rid of it. She wants it to be perfect.

Similarly, as Christians—the bride of Christ—we need to prepare ourselves to meet Jesus—the bridegroom—by making sure we are pure and spotless. Of course we will never be perfect while living on this earth, but we can attain toward it. Just as the bride is quick to remove any spot or blemish from her white gown, we too must be quick to cleanse our souls by repenting when we have sinned. It is because of the love of the bridegroom, His death for us on the cross, that we can be made pure and spotless. Paul states in the book of Ephesians, "...Husbands love your wives, just as Christ loved the church and gave Himself up for her to make her holy...and to present her to Himself...without stain or wrinkle or any other blemish."4

A month ago God gave me a dream in which I was at a wedding banquet! (I later realized that it was *the* wedding banquet!) I saw my girlfriend of thirty years come to sit at the banquet table. I had led her to the Lord only a year before. My first thought was how beautiful she looked, dressed in a white wedding gown with pastel flowers stitched into the bodice. I then looked to my left and saw my friend who was like a brother to me. I had prayed with him only months before for the healing of a torn aorta in his heart. God gave him a miracle by keeping him from death. He appeared in my dream to be very refined, dressed is his wedding attire of a suit and bow tie. As I continued to walk around the banquet, I came upon others whom I knew, prayed for, and ministered to "in the natural." My eyes fell upon a woman whom I had been ministering to as of late. This former drug addict and prostitute was radiant in her wedding gown, also with flowers in the bodice, but of different colors than the first. My dream ended without ever seeing the bridegroom. It was as if we were all waiting for him to arrive.

All of the people that I saw in my dream were still alive and had received salvation through Jesus Christ. It was His blood that was poured out on the cross that took the sins of each one, including the prostitute. Would some have been surprised to see a prostitute at the banquet and wearing a white dress, symbolizing purity? God has me ministering to many like her, and as I do, He reveals to me how He sees them—as beautiful brides dressed in white. Once these women said yes to Jesus, they were washed in the Savior's blood. Their sins were forgiven and forgotten. To Him they are His brides and He says to them... "Arise, My beloved, My beautiful one and come with me!"[5]

"I saw the Holy City, the new Jerusalem,
coming down out of heaven from God,
prepared as a bride beautifully
dressed for her husband."
Revelation 21:2

Notes

1. John 4:1-26
2. Song of Solomon 2 and 3
3. Matthew 22:2
4. Ephesians 5:25-27
5. Song of Solomon 2:10

"Whatever you did for one of the
least of these brothers and sisters
of Mine, you did for Me."
Matthew 25:40

Chapter Nine

Feed My Sheep

Jesus asked "Do you love Me?" "Yes, Lord, I do love you." He asked again "Do you love Me?" "Yes, Lord, you know that I love you." He asked yet a third time, "Do you love Me?" A third time came the reply "Lord, you know all things—you know that I love you." Jesus responded, "Feed my sheep." I hear my Lord, the One whom I profess to love, tell me these same words, the ones that He told Peter in the Bible.[1]

I sat there in the church, warm and cozy, with my hands stretched high. My heart is sincere when it cries out to God, "I love you Lord! I love you with my whole heart, with my whole mind, and with my whole being!" I then have a vision...I see the four walls of the church building fall out and open like the sides of a cardboard box. I proceed to walk out of the church, and into the street where I meet people who have chains around their wrists. I take the keys that are in my hands and I unlock their chains so that they are set free.

I had another vision that I was a shepherd who went out into the field to look for the lost sheep. I came upon one sheep that was caught in some barbed wire, so I bent down to help it get free. I gathered up the slightly wounded sheep into my arms when I spotted another sheep that was in the mouth of a wolf. I got angry when I saw its fangs sunk into my precious sheep. I ran to the rescue of my sheep and scared off the preying wolf with my staff. I then picked up my scared and wounded sheep and joined it with the other. I proceeded to take them back to the fold where I bound up their wounds so that they were healed. I fed them, gave them water to drink, and looked after them so that they were safe. Jesus said, "If you love Me, then feed my sheep."[2] It is true that in the Bible Jesus is depicted as "the good Shepherd,"[3] but He also calls us to be like Him and to follow Him; so as to do as He does.

On another occasion Jesus told the disciples, "For I was hungry and you gave me something to eat, I was thirsty and you gave me something to drink, I was a stranger and you invited Me in, I needed clothes and you clothed Me, I was sick and you looked after Me, I was in prison and you came to visit Me...Truly I tell you, whatever you did for one of the least of these brothers and sisters of Mine, you did for Me."[3] If I profess to love Jesus, then I need to show it not only in my words but in my actions. He doesn't mind hearing the words from me, especially if they are sincere, but His greatest desire is that I show Him my love by loving others—those whom He calls His sheep.

When I wake up each morning I ask God to let me be His hands, feet and mouthpiece. I ask Him to use me as His vessel of love. I ask Him to lead me in that day...What I am to do, where I am to go, whom He wants me to talk to, and what He would have me say. I ask Him to let me see others with His eyes and to hear them with His ears. I ask Him to give to me His heart, so that I am filled with His feelings, His desires, and His thoughts. I also want to be filled with His power and His glory so I ask Holy Spirit to fill me afresh. When I step out of my house each day and into the streets where darkness and evil may be present, I want to be a force of love and light that overcomes it. I never know who the Lord will bring into my path or what He might ask me to do.

One morning while in church, a young couple came through the doors. I introduced myself to the male who shared that he and his girlfriend were living in a tent close to the church. I was horrified at the thought of living in a tent especially because winter was fast approaching, and the temperatures in the evenings were as low as forty degrees. It so happened that I brought them to my home that day with the intention of driving them to a homeless shelter on the following day. When morning arrived, my husband and I did not feel it in our hearts to drop them off at a shelter in the center of the city where there was known to be a lot of crime.

For eight days straight, we sought the Lord, waking each morning with the question "What do you want us to do with them today?" As each day passed, we loved them, fed them, prayed with them and taught them the Word of God. We treated them as our very own family. We were open to keeping the young woman but God revealed to us that it wasn't His plan. On the eighth day, two doors opened—one for her—an old school friend invited her to live in her home. And one for him—an aunt and uncle invited him to stay with them. Afterwards, when our home was quiet and still, I felt that God was saying that

He used me to rescue them. What they were rescued from exactly, I am not certain. What I do know is that with each new day, I asked Him to lead me; to equip me and to use me for His purposes. I believe that God did have His way in me, and it was for His glory.

There is another momentous occasion when I saw God's glory manifest before my eyes. I woke up that day with the intention of having my son's friend over the house for a play date. They met in the summer at a Christian summer camp in a town close by. When the boy was dropped over, I invited his mother whom I had met previously, to stay and visit for a while. In our conversation she shared of a circumstance in her life that was worrisome to her and involved her daughter. I asked her if she would like me to pray for her right then. The woman whom I knew was saved, bowed her head to receive prayer.

As I sought the Lord for the words to pray, I felt that He wanted her to receive the fullness of His Spirit through the baptism of the Holy Spirit. She accepted God's invitation and so I acted as God's conduit—His hands and mouthpiece—and beckoned Him for His power and words to flow through me and into her. Tears began to flow like a water faucet from her eyes. She excused herself for the display of tears, but she said that she just wasn't able to contain them. She told me that she felt His presence through warm and tingling feelings in her body. She also shared with me that there was something that morning that was telling her that she shouldn't go to my home but she fought it and became determined to go. It was at that moment that she realized that God had a glorious plan for her that day that the devil tried to thwart. She and I both prayed upon waking that God have His way in our lives, and He did!

I can sit on my cushioned chair in the comfort of my church and profess my love to God twenty-four hours a day. I can lift my empty hands to the air to express the depth of my love for Him. I can dance around the church, filled with the joy of His presence...But if I do not go out of the church building and take His presence and love to others...If I do not take my feet into the streets and reach out with my hands to the lost, the hungry, and the broken, then He will say to me on judgment day, "Depart from me, you who are cursed; into the eternal fire prepared for the devil and his angels. For I was hungry and you gave me nothing to eat, I was thirsty and you gave me nothing to drink, I was a stranger and you did not invite me in, I needed clothes and you did not clothe me, I was sick and in prison and you did not look after me."[5] My heart's desire is to hear Jesus say to me on judgment day, "Come, you who are blessed by my Father; take your inheritance, the kingdom prepared for you since the creation of the world."[6]

Forgive me Lord for being selfish. I've acted as a spoiled child and have demanded "Give me more Lord!" You will only give me more as I give away what you've already given. Forgive me for wasting the time and talents that you've given to me. Let me not waste another moment. Let me heed your command to "Go out into all the world and preach the gospel to all creation."[7]

"As I have loved you, so you must
love one another. By this, everyone will
know that you are my disciples,
if you love one another."
John 13:34, 35

[81]

Notes

1. John 21:15-17
2. John 21:17
3. John 10:11
4. Matthew 25:35-40
5. Matthew 25:41
6. Matthew 25:34
7. Mark 16:15

"And now these three remain: faith, hope and love.
But the greatest of these is love."
1 Corinthians 13:13

Chapter Ten

The Greatest of these is Love

I was laying there squirming in my skin. This wasn't a comfortable feeling. I didn't like it. I felt useless, as if I had no value at all. I recently was forced to leave my job as house mother at a home for unwed mothers. I wasn't able to teach Sunday school to the first graders or feed the hungry at the weekly soup kitchen. I wasn't able to stand on the altar and read the Bible readings on Sunday mornings, nor was I able to sidewalk counsel at the local abortion clinic. I was useless lying in my bed, day in and day out, ever since I had a nervous breakdown.

Everything changed on the day that I got a revelation while attending a weekend retreat. The Biblical account of the sisters of Lazarus, Mary and Martha, was the focus.[1] I had imagined in my mind's eye Mary sitting at the feet of Jesus, whom she loved with all of her heart. Martha was going about, busying herself, trying to gain the reputation as "the hostess with the mostess." She was trying to gain the approval and love of Jesus by her actions, but Jesus said in response to this, "Mary has chosen the better thing."[2] It was then that God revealed to me that He loved me just as I am; that I didn't need to do anything to win His love, nor did I need to prove to Him that I was worth loving. He was telling me that even if I just lay in bed all day and night and did nothing, that He loved me. He loved me no less then, than when I ran about doing ministry work seven days a week.

We must get a revelation of who we are in Christ. We are the BELOVED sons and daughters of God. We must know that we are loved before we try going out to spread the gospel to others...Because everything we do must be motivated by love. If I do not feed the homeless woman in the food kitchen because I have love for her in my heart, but I do it to prove that I am good and valuable, than she will feel that my intention to help her is not because I care for her. She will know that what I'm doing is out of selfish motives. If I do not feed her without showing her the love of God, then the reason for my being there has no value in the kingdom of God because God's sole desire is that she come to know Him and receive the gift of salvation. How will the lost that I minister to know Him, unless I act like Him, talk like Him, and love like Him. I cannot portray the love of God to others without knowing His love first. I cannot pour it out without first being filled with it.

My number one prayer these past twenty-five years has been, "Fill me with Your love God." And let me tell you, He has been answering this prayer. I know it because it is His love that has moved me to pray over the cripple that he walk and run without hindrance. It was His love that moved me to take into my home a homeless couple. It was His love that moved me to help heal the hearts of abused women in my workshops. It was His love that moved me to command devils to leave the woman who was being mentally tormented. God allows me to see the lost, the sinful, the angry and hardened, the broken and abused, the dirty and smelly—with His eyes. He allows me to feel the pain that He feels in His heart for each one. I have literally felt my heart break for ones that He has brought before me.

It is out of His love that His power flows from me and brings supernatural healing and deliverance to others. It is out of His love that words of prophecy come from my mouth and touch the hearts of the ones with whom I speak with. It is out of His love that I lead the sinner to repentance and to

[87]

receive salvation through Jesus Christ. Healing, prophecy, wisdom, words of knowledge, miracles...These are gifts of the Spirit[3] that we ought to be mindful of and desire to have, as they are tools to help encourage and edify others. However, if I do not utilize these God-given tools from the motivation of love and compassion, then they become just show pieces—"Look what I can do. Look at my gifts."

What I seek most is not the gifts of the Spirit, but the fruits of the Spirit.[4] Every day I pray to God to fill me up to overflowing with His fruits of love, peace, joy, patience, gentleness, kindness...If I am being patient, gentle or kind to a person, then I am loving them. If I am in the midst of a storm in my life, and remember that I am loved by a good Father who works all things out for my good, then I can hold on to my peace and joy. This becomes a witness to non-believers around me and it causes them to desire to know the love of God as I have.

Paul in the Bible urges us to desire the gifts of the Spirit, but he adds "Yet, I will show you a more excellent way."[5] The more excellent way is LOVE. In the chapter known as the "Love Chapter,"[6] Paul explains that if he possessed all of the gifts but had not love then he was nothing and gained nothing. "If I have the gift of prophecy...and if I have a faith that can move mountains, but do not have love, I am nothing. If I give all I possess to the poor and give over my body to hardship that I may boast, but do not have love, I gain nothing."[7] I can raise the dead and cause blind eyes to see, but if I do not have love, I gain nothing. I can teach great mysteries of God and possess much wisdom, but if I do not have love, I am nothing. I can preach amazing sermons and publish a dozen books in my lifetime, but if I have not done it all in love, I have gained nothing.

To sum up my thoughts, I will end with Paul's final words of the Love Chapter: "And now these three remain: faith, hope and love. But the greatest of these is love."[8]

"And over all these, put on love."
Colossians 3:14

Notes

1. Luke 10:38-42
2. Mark 12:31
3. 1 Corinthians 12:7-11 (Nine gifts)
4. Galatians 5:22,23 (Nine fruits)
5. 1 Corinthians 12:31
6. 1 Corinthians 13
7. 1 Corinthians 13:2,3
8. 1 Corinthians 13:13

*"Beloved, let us love one another, for love
is from God, and whoever loves has been
born of God and knows God."*
1 John 4:7

Afterword

Vessels of God's Love
(True stories)

Poster Child for the Glory of God

I looked into this sixty-seven year old man's face and saw the face of a young boy that was lit up with joy, as if he had received every item on his Christmas list. His loving Father healed his body—gave him mobility to run and jump, and raise his arms toward the heavens in praise!

He had fallen three times in the days prior, even with the use of a cane. As a child, he was known as the poster boy for the March of Dimes because he suffered the effects of a horrible disease called polio. He spent all of his life crippled. His parents spent all of their lives crying out to God to heal their son. His wife joined in the efforts to bombard heaven. She knew that in heaven lived a merciful God, One who gives good gifts to His children; One, who like any loving father, doesn't wish pain or sickness upon them.

The prayers did not fall on deaf ears. He was told that he would never walk. He walked at age four. He was told that he would never have vision good enough to apply for a driver's license. He received his license at age forty. He was told that he would never be able to hold a job. He was employed by the state from the age of eighteen through the age of forty-eight. At age fifty-nine he was in a coma and the doctors said that he wouldn't live. During his visit to heaven, his mother told him that it wasn't his time yet. At age sixty-seven, while praying in a church, His loving, ever-mindful Father reached down from heaven to bless his faithful son with another gift...

He slowly wobbled into church, leaning heavily on his cane; praying that he wouldn't fall a fourth time in a single week. While there, a sister in the Lord leaned over to bless him. Suddenly, God's healing love flowed into his body. Glory to God! He didn't leave the same way that he came in! Before exiting the church, he jumped up and down, and ran around the church ten times. When he arrived at his home, he placed his cane in the coat closet and then ran up and down a flight of stairs; the same stairs that he fell on only one day before.

Hershey Kisses

She said that she liked the Hershey Kisses that I gave her. Was it the bag of candy I gave her or the book with the vignette that I wrote called "Hershey Kisses?" It describes how our loving Father gives us gifts to reveal His love to His children...

She had just walked away from a life of drug addiction. She traveled across country to a "foreign land," to start a new life, knowing that she needed His power to overcome her past. She walked into the Christ-centered home shaking visibly from anxiety, only to look upon a face that she knew from her hometown. How could that be? She learned that her friend had moved left their home state to move to New York, who later moved to Boston, who then moved to the same home where the two just met. Did God orchestrate all of that just for her—brought a remnant from home to make her feel welcomed and comforted in one of the most stressful moments of her life? You bet He did! And why couldn't He? He is the same big God who created the world and everything in it. And why wouldn't He? He is the same God who created her and adopted her to be His own child.

Laid-Down Lover

She loves and is loved by the One who is love. He pours His love into her heart and it overflows into others. She is a laid-down lover for Him; a vessel of His love to be poured out on the "unloved" and "unlovable." His love caused her to take into her own home four "broken" women throughout the course of six months. Just when one moved on to go forward on her journey, another one would come along hoping for a "love-handout." Freely she receives, so freely she gives...

This laid-down lover wept as she received a gift from her loving Father. She had cried out to her Daddy to "give to her her daily bread" for three long weeks. In the place where she gave shelter and love to the ones in need, she was three weeks past due with the rent. She was expecting an eviction notice from the landlord any day, but she was also expecting Her Daddy to provide manna from heaven. And He did! He provided more than enough to pay her rent through the generosity of an old friend—also a vessel of God's love.

Like Job

Even atheists know the story of Job in the Bible; the story of the man whom God allowed Satan to take everything from; except his life. Her life reminds me of the life of Job. She is only fifty years old, but she sits in a wheelchair, residing in a nursing home. She lost her health, her ministry, her home, and her personal belongings. She doesn't have her family either, but she does have a loving Father who says that she is the apple of His eye, and who has her name carved in the palm of His hand...

I heard her giggle like a care-free little girl. I had never heard that sound come from her lips. She couldn't contain the joy inside as she opened the two brown packages that just got delivered to her lap. She pulled out a pink, warm and fuzzy bathrobe, two pairs of pajamas, slippers, and a journal filled with God's promises. They were gifts from above—a sign of her Father's love. I watched her put on her new robe, and as she did, I imagined the Father wrapping His big, warm arms of love around her to let her know that she is safe and in His care. I watched her open the journal and read the words from the Giver of the gifts... "I know the plans I have for you; plans for your welfare and not for woe; plans to give you a future full of hope." You might've guessed that there had to be someone who the Father used to deliver those gifts to her, and you would be right. A woman from church sent them—not a family relative, nor a close friend—but a vessel of the Father's love.

The Scribe

I just had to tell others about how good our God is! It was exploding inside of me—the need to tell of His great love! I don't have a pulpit to preach from or a microphone on a stage. What I do have is this laptop, and so these words are bursting from my heart and onto the printed page. Each one of these four stories is a first-hand account. I gazed into the eyes of each one—each child of God. I listened to the cries and the laughter of each one. I witnessed the light and the joy that filled their faces when they received their heavenly gifts and recognized that they were not forgotten; that they were indeed loved by God. Within each of these stories, it is important to emphasize that God didn't work alone. He needed people to offer themselves as vessels of His love. He needed people who were willing to be His hands and feet; His eyes, mouth and ears. He needed people willing to give whatever it was that He asked them to give—whether it was their time, their money, their home, their talent or their prayers. He needed people willing to give from their hearts.

Prayer

My prayer for the reader...

"I pray that you, being rooted and established
in love, may have power, together with all the
Lord's holy people, to grasp how wide and long and
high and deep is the love of Christ,
and to know this love that surpasses knowledge—
that you may be filled to the
measure of all the fullness of God."
Ephesians 3:17-19

A prayer from your heart to God...

Holy Spirit, fill me to overflowing with the fruit of
Your presence—that which is love. Pour into my
heart Your hot liquid love that it may melt the
hardened places of my heart, and be as a healing
balm to the wounds in my heart. I pray that as I am
filled with Your love, I will love You in return with
my whole heart, mind and strength. May Your love
overflow from my heart and into those around me. I
am making the choice to join Your army of laid-
down lovers. I want to be a son/daughter of Your
revolution of love. Amen.

Other Books
by Holly Otten

The Tin Man-
The Voice of an Incest Survivor

hand in Hand-
A True Life Story

Free to Dance

Brides of Christ

Available at Amazon.com in paperback and
ebook. Also at www.tinmanministries.com/store

Made in the USA
Lexington, KY
22 November 2019